Original title:

Love's Resurgence

Copyright © 2024 Swan Charm

Author: Liina Liblikas

ISBN HARDBACK: 978-9916-89-196-4

ISBN PAPERBACK: 978-9916-89-197-1

ISBN EBOOK: 978-9916-89-198-8

The Art of Starting Anew

With each sunrise, a fresh embrace,
The past behind, we find our place.
Chasing dreams, with hearts set free,
In every step, we dare to see.

Old shadows fade, as hope ignites,
We mend our wings, prepare for flights.
Through storms we rise, with steadfast will,
A canvas blank, our dreams to fill.

Faded Letters Come to Life

In dusty drawers, they lie in wait,
Words of love, entwined by fate.
A gentle breeze, a whisper's call,
Revives the tales we've shared with all.

Each ink-stained page, a story spills,
Of laughter, dreams, and youthful thrills.
From time-worn scripts, new visions flow,
Faded letters, with love's soft glow.

In the Cocoon of Togetherness

We weave our lives like threads in gold,
In the warmth of arms, we're never cold.
Through laughter shared and tears unspooled,
In this cocoon, our hearts are fueled.

With every heartbeat, dreams align,
A sanctuary, your hand in mine.
In stillness found, our spirits grow,
Together, forever, our love's sweet flow.

From Ashes to Awakening

From embers glows a spark divine,
A journey starts, a life reclaim.
With every breath, we start anew,
From ashes rise, with skies so blue.

The past will speak, but it won't bind,
With strength we seek, and peace we find.
Hope ignites, as shadows fade,
In resilience, our future's laid.

The Lantern of Rekindled Sentiments

In twilight's glow, old memories alight,
Whispers of love, soft as the night.
The lantern burns bright, illuminating the past,
Moments we cherish, forever to last.

Flickering shadows dance on the wall,
Each flicker a story, a whispering call.
Hearts intertwined through the ebb and flow,
Rekindled fires, igniting the glow.

Essence of Yesterday's Hopes

A sigh of the wind through the trees,
Carries the echoes of dreams with ease.
Yesterday's hopes in the warmth of the sun,
Promises made that will never be done.

Each droplet of rain holds a tale of the past,
Reflections of moments, serene and steadfast.
With every sunrise, new chances arise,
Essence of dreams, painted in skies.

Resurgence of Shared Laughter

Laughter erupts like a springtime bloom,
Filling the air, dispersing all gloom.
In echoes of joy, we find our way back,
Resurgence of moments we thought we lack.

Through trials and time, our spirits align,
Shared laughter grows, a love so divine.
The heart sings a tune, familiar and bright,
A melody woven in the shimmering light.

A Heartbeat of Reunited Dreams

In the hush of the night, dreams softly entwine,
A heartbeat resounds, a rhythm divine.
Reunited paths under the starlit sky,
Whispers of wishes that never say die.

Together we stand, with hope in our eyes,
Chasing the dawn as the old darkness dies.
In the embrace of tomorrow, our futures gleam,
Fueled by the power of reunited dreams.

Threads of Destiny Rewoven

In the loom of time we weave,
Our dreams with threads we believe.
Each color speaks of paths untold,
In patterns bright, our fates unfold.

Whispers of the past arise,
With each stitch, a sweet surprise.
Bound by hopes and dreams we share,
Together woven, a tapestry rare.

With hands entwined, we trace the lines,
Of destinies that entwine.
In the fabric of our lives we find,
The hearts connected, combined.

As the daylight softly fades,
New designs in twilight shades.
Through laughter, tears, we interlace,
In life's rich tapestry, we find our place.

So let us craft with care and love,
The threads of fate from stars above.
For in this tapestry we'll see,
The beauty of our unity.

The Lilt of Longing Hearts

In the quiet night we sigh,
Hearts that whisper, feeling shy.
Melodies of dreams take flight,
As stars above ignite the night.

Every glance, a silent plea,
Two souls yearning to be free.
With every beat, the echoes start,
The haunting lilt of longing hearts.

In the moonlight's gentle glow,
Secrets only lovers know.
Between the beats, love's gentle spark,
Guiding through the night so dark.

Through the shadows, hope will gleam,
In tender moments, we will dream.
Together in this dance, we'll part,
Forever bound by longing hearts.

As dawn breaks, we hold on tight,
To the promises of the night.
Yet in the light, hope departs,
But lingers still, longing hearts.

A Mending Serenade

In twilight's arms, we softly mend,
With whispered notes, our hearts suspend.
Each chord a promise, each tune a balm,
Creating peace, a tender calm.

Through storms of doubt, we find our way,
In melodies that gently sway.
With every strum, the pain recedes,
As love's sweet song fulfills our needs.

We gather close beneath the stars,
Our hearts unlace from all the scars.
The music weaves through night's embrace,
A serenade of love's warm grace.

In harmony, we lift and rise,
Two souls entwined beneath the skies.
Each note a thread, our souls connect,
In this mending, we reflect.

Let the serenade play on soft,
A healing touch, a gentle croft.
Through every phrase, together stand,
In the symphony of love, so grand.

Mirrors of Shared Shadows

In darkened rooms where secrets glow,
Reflections dance, two souls in tow.
Shadows whisper of paths intertwined,
Mirrors show the hearts aligned.

In quiet corners, we confront,
The fears and dreams that we recount.
Each echo shapes the life we share,
In mirrored depths, a bond laid bare.

Beyond the glass, illusions fade,
In every laugh, a truth displayed.
Together, we embrace the light,
In shadows cast, we find our sight.

So let us wander through the night,
In mirrored hearts, a shared delight.
With open arms, our spirits blend,
In shadows' arms, our love transcends.

Through every mirror that we meet,
We learn to dance to love's heartbeat.
In shared reflections, we will find,
The beautiful depths of hearts combined.

Beneath the Surface

Whispers hide in depths below,
Secrets only shadows know.
Ripples dance like fleeting dreams,
Life, it breathes in silent streams.

Hidden truths in waters deep,
Stories lost that silence keeps.
Glimmers spark a hidden light,
Awakening the dark of night.

Piercing through the veils of time,
Echoed calls, a distant chime.
Underneath where thoughts collide,
Beneath the surface, hopes abide.

A Current Stirs

A gentle flow begins to rise,
Softly sweeping through the skies.
With every shift, the world awakes,
A quiet force, the stillness breaks.

Whirling dreams in currents swirl,
Whispers of a longing girl.
Braided paths where wishes thread,
Above the chaos, hearts are fed.

Through the rush, a pulse of grace,
Embracing life in every space.
As waters churn, so spirits soar,
A current stirs, forevermore.

Orchard of Forgotten Promises

In shadows of an ancient tree,
Lies the past, wild and free.
Branches stretch with tales untold,
Of dreams once bright that turned to gold.

Faded petals lost to time,
Rustling leaves in turn to rhyme.
Whispers weave through fragrant air,
In this place, love's memories share.

Beneath the boughs, we find our way,
Through echoes of a brighter day.
An orchard filled with sweet regret,
Where shadows linger, hearts won't forget.

The Gentle Stir of Affection

Softly brushing past the skin,
A warmth that brews from deep within.
Eyelids flutter, hearts take flight,
In tender moments, pure delight.

Fingers graze in silent dance,
A breathless touch, a fleeting glance.
As laughter twirls on breezy nights,
The gentle stir of sweet delights.

In every sigh, an unspoken bond,
Where feelings linger, love responds.
With every heartbeat, echoes ring,
Through each soft whisper, memories cling.

Radiance from the Ashes of the Past

From gray remains, new life emerges,
A phoenix born; the heart surges.
Old wounds heal in candlelight,
Guided by stars in the night.

Embers glow with whispered hope,
Through darkest times, we learn to cope.
The past may crumble, fade away,
Yet love transforms, finds its way.

Bright blossoms rise from lifeless ground,
In every loss, a strength is found.
Radiant souls, our stories cast,
From ashes strewn, we rise at last.

Vows Written in Starry Skies

Beneath the glow of ancient stars,
We whisper dreams that travel far.
Promises cast in silver light,
Our hearts entwined, a wondrous sight.

The cosmos holds our tender words,
In silken threads of time, unheard.
With every twinkle, love's embrace,
Together, we find our sacred space.

The night unveils our silent pact,
In guiding moons, our souls intact.
Through constellations, we'll explore,
Upon this path, forevermore.

When shadows fall and doubts arise,
We'll seek the truth in starlit skies.
Hand in hand, we rise and soar,
With vows that bind us evermore.

As dawn approaches, dreams take flight,
In every day, we find our light.
Together, under sun and shade,
Our love's foundation is embraced.

Writing Chapters Unfinished

Pages turn with gentle grace,
Each word a step, a fleeting trace.
Stories woven, threads unspun,
A journey shared, two lives as one.

Ink runs deep in wishes penned,
In every line, our hearts unbend.
With hopes and fears, we lay it bare,
In unfinished tales, love's sweet care.

The chapters linger, yet to write,
With every dawn, new dreams ignite.
As time unfolds, we grasp the pen,
To shape the future, again and again.

Amidst the lines, our laughter flows,
In whispered dreams, our true heart knows.
Each pause, a breath, a moment's sigh,
Together we forge, as days pass by.

For every tale, a twist anew,
With ink and love, we'll see it through.
In every pause, a chance to rise,
We'll write our fate beneath the skies.

The Tide of Togetherness Returns

Waves crash softly on the shore,
A dance of love we can't ignore.
With every ebb, we find our way,
In tides that speak what words can't say.

Our bond, a current, strong and true,
Guiding us in all we do.
As seashells whisper tales of old,
We weave our dreams, in heartbeats bold.

Together, we rise with the sun,
In harmony, we are as one.
Each moment shared, a treasure found,
In rhythms deep where love abounds.

Through storms that test, we stand so firm,
In every challenge, hearts still churn.
The tide may pull, but we remain,
In unity, we break through pain.

The ocean sings, a soothing song,
In this embrace, we both belong.
As laughter dances on the breeze,
Together, life flows with such ease.

The Gift of Second Chances

Beneath the weight of past regrets,
We search for paths our heart begets.
With every stumble, lessons learned,
In second chances, hope is burned.

A fractured soul, exploring light,
In shadows cast, we find our might.
With open hearts, we start again,
Embracing change, we rise, defend.

In whispered dreams, the past shall fade,
From ashes, new beginnings made.
For every scar, a story told,
A treasure held in love's strong hold.

With tender hands, we shape our fate,
In every moment, we await.
Together walking, side by side,
In grace, we mend, in love, abide.

The gift of time, a gentle grace,
In every heartbeat, love we trace.
For in each chance, our spirits soar,
A journey vast, forevermore.

Secrets of the Heart Revived

In whispers soft, the feelings dwell,
Locked away, a silent spell.
Time has passed, yet sparks remain,
In quiet corners, love's refrain.

Through shadows deep, the heart takes flight,
Rekindled dreams in soft moonlight.
The past revives with gentle grace,
A tender touch, a warm embrace.

Like old friends found on a rainy day,
Memories dance, they find their way.
With open arms, we welcome back,
The secrets lost along the track.

Each heartbeat whispers, truths to share,
In every corner, a hidden care.
Revived once more, the flame ignites,
In softest hues, love's purest sights.

In sacred spaces, our souls align,
Unearthed desires in sunlit time.
Through trials faced, we rise and meet,
The secrets of our hearts, complete.

Singing to the Ghosts of Affection

In haunted halls, their melodies soar,
Echoes of love that once swore,
In twilight's glow, the shadows sway,
Singing softly of yesterday.

Each whispered note a tender sigh,
For moments lost that never die.
Vibrations linger in the air,
A haunting tune, beyond compare.

With every chord, the heart takes flight,
Balancing joy with bitter night.
The ghosts of affection still remain,
In every laugh, in every pain.

Through verses spun of joy and grief,
We find solace in sweet belief.
Singing to shadows, we embrace,
The lingering touch of love's grace.

In twilight's dance, our voices blend,
To broken hearts, we find our mend.
With every song, we let them go,
Singing softly, yet feeling so.

Remnants of Paint on Old Canvas

The colors fade, yet stories stand,
Whispers trapped in a painter's hand.
Brush strokes linger, true and bold,
Capturing tales that need retold.

Textures wear with time's embrace,
Textures hint at a lost grace.
In every hue, a life once felt,
Memories bound through art's own belt.

Each layer tells of joy and strife,
The remnants of a vivid life.
With every glance, the heart can see,
The beauty held in history.

In quiet rooms where shades collide,
The past unfolds, and tears subside.
Painted dreams on canvas lay,
Whispers of love in shades of gray.

In every stroke, a story waits,
To break the silence that time creates.
Remnants cherished, colors found,
In art's embrace, our hearts unbound.

The Echoes of Unsaid Words

In silence thick, our hearts converse,
Unfinished thoughts, a hidden verse.
The echoes linger in the air,
A tapestry of unvoiced care.

Each moment lost to fear of fate,
Words left untouched, we hesitate.
In shadows deep, the truth awaits,
A whispered wish that time abates.

With every glance, confessions hide,
Between the lines, our hearts collide.
The echoes of what might have been,
In every pause, a subtle din.

Yet in the stillness, a spark ignites,
To serve as guide through darkened nights.
The unsaid flows beneath the skin,
A river wide where feelings swim.

In the quietude, we find our grace,
As echoes linger, we embrace.
The unsaid words shall take their flight,
Transforming silence into light.

Euphoria in Gala of Reunions

Laughter echoes in the air,
Faces gleam with joy to share.
Old friends gather, time stands still,
Hearts unite with warm goodwill.

Memories dance in every smile,
Moments cherished, worth the while.
Underneath the starlit sky,
We celebrate, no need to cry.

Stories told with a gentle laugh,
Time rewinds, we live the past.
Connections felt in every glance,
Life's sweet tune sings us to dance.

With every hug, the world feels light,
In this space, everything feels right.
Together, we weave our fate,
In this gala, we celebrate.

A night to cherish, to recall,
In unity, we stand tall.
Euphoria wraps us like a quilt,
A heart's reunion, love rebuilt.

Secrets Carried by the Whispering Breeze

Breezes whisper through the trees,
Carrying tales, soft like leaves.
In the quiet, secrets flow,
Nature's voice begins to sow.

A gentle touch, a fleeting sigh,
Underneath the vast, blue sky.
The wind knows all, it softly speaks,
Of hidden dreams and weary peaks.

Each gust brings stories to the shore,
From high mountains to ocean's roar.
In its embrace, we find release,
The whispers bring a sense of peace.

As twilight wraps the world in grace,
The breeze unveils a sacred space.
Listen close, let worries cease,
In the silence, find your peace.

Secrets linger in the night,
Carried forth in gentle flight.
Through the dark, let your heart seize,
The magic held by whispered breeze.

Reclaimed Melodies of Connected Souls

In echoes sweet, our voices blend,
Harmonies that never end.
Together, we find our lost refrain,
In every note, love's sweet pain.

Melodies woven through the years,
Filling hearts, dissolving fears.
Every heartbeat, every sigh,
In a song, we learn to fly.

Connected souls with dreams to share,
In rhythms strong, we lay bare.
Notes like whispers in the air,
In this symphony, we find care.

And as the world outside may fade,
In every chord, we're unafraid.
Unity wrapped in every sound,
In reclaimed joy, our hearts are found.

A song for those who choose to see,
The beauty in our harmony.
Together we stand, strong and whole,
Reclaimed melodies of the soul.

In the Garden of Reclaimed Emotions

In silent blooms, our hearts awake,
Tender petals, a soft ache.
Colors bright, a vivid scene,
In this garden, we find our sheen.

Memories planted, roots so deep,
In every flower, stories keep.
Love and loss, they weave and twine,
In the soil, our hearts do shine.

Fragrances of laughter and tears,
Whispers echo through the years.
Each bloom tells of times we've shared,
In this sanctuary, we've dared.

Growth emerges from every pain,
As sunlight kisses drops of rain.
Nurtured under skies so bright,
In this garden, we find light.

Reclaimed emotions, tender grace,
In every corner, a safe space.
Together, let our spirits soar,
In this garden, forevermore.

Memories Blossoming in Quiet Corners

In shadows where whispers dwell,
Old laughter hangs like a bell.
Among the books and dust we find,
Fleeting dreams, our hearts entwined.

Petals fall from time's embrace,
Softly weaving through this space.
Each moment dances, bright yet frail,
In hidden nooks, our tales unveil.

A cup of tea, a gentle sigh,
Echoes of days that flutter by.
The scent of love, both sweet and mild,
Recalls the spirit of a child.

Beneath the branches, secrets rest,
The tiny joys we once confessed.
They bloom anew in quiet light,
As memories take graceful flight.

In every corner, shadows play,
While sunlight spills, a warm ballet.
We cherish moments softly spun,
In quiet corners, we are one.

The Sweet Surrender of Second Chances

With every heartbeat, hope arises,
From ashes bloom surprise disguises.
A fleeting glance, a tender smile,
Our broken paths meet for a while.

The gentle rain, it washes pain,
Like soothing balm, a sweet refrain.
In open arms, we let love sway,
Embracing dawn, the light of day.

Each stumble brings a lesson learned,
A spark of grace, the heart discerned.
We dance on dreams, though shadows creep,
In second chances, love runs deep.

With every turn, a new embrace,
A canvas brushed with fate's own grace.
Past sorrows fade, like distant songs,
As we absorb where hope belongs.

In whispered vows, we find our place,
A story woven, time and space.
The sweet surrender, soft and grand,
Unfolding gently, hand in hand.

A Tapestry of New Beginnings

Threads of color intertwine,
Each hue a memory, a sign.
Rising sun wakes seeds of thought,
In every stitch, new dreams are wrought.

A canvas spread beneath the skies,
Bold strokes of joy where freedom lies.
Hope unfurls with every breath,
In the embrace of life and death.

The winding road leads us away,
Yet beckons on with each new day.
With laughter shared and tears set free,
We weave together you and me.

Blooming gardens, hearts awake,
New beginnings, paths we take.
In every moment, colors blend,
As life's rich tapestry does mend.

So let us journey, hand in hand,
Through fields of dreams, upon this land.
In every chapter, love's refrain,
We find the beauty in the pain.

Remnants of a Lost Symphony

In quiet halls where echoes fade,
Remnants of dreams, a serenade.
Once vibrant notes scatter like leaves,
Now stitched together in what deceives.

Fingers trace the dusty score,
Memories dance on the wooden floor.
In the silence, musings linger,
Each heartbeat pulses like a singer.

The heart remembers every tune,
Whispers of joy, the light of moon.
Yet shadows hold the notes undone,
In every chord, we feel what's spun.

A melody that's carved in time,
Woven whispers, a wistful rhyme.
In shadows deep, the past will twine,
Lost symphonies, their truths align.

From silence bursts a hopeful cry,
New songs arise in every sigh.
Though remnants of the old may fade,
In every end, new paths are laid.

In the Garden of Lost Affections

Petals whisper secrets lost,
In shadows memories hum,
Faded dreams on trellis frost,
Where love once blossomed, now it's numb.

Silent echoes wander wide,
Among the flowers of despair,
Time's cruel hands cannot abide,
Yet still, I linger, seek you there.

Branches bend with aching grace,
Yearning for a touch once near,
In this quiet, sacred space,
Your laughter lingers, soft and clear.

Among the weeds, a hope may bloom,
Yet thorns remind of paths not taken,
In every breath, a trace of gloom,
Yet somewhere, love remains unshaken.

Beneath the stars, beneath the trees,
Breathless sighs of what could be,
In the garden, heart's unease,
For you, I cultivate my plea.

Intertwined Paths of Rediscovery

Two roads cross beneath the sky,
Once we walked them, hand in hand,
Memories linger, never die,
In whispered moments, we still stand.

Footprints fade in sands of time,
Yet the echoes still remain,
In every heartbeat, every rhyme,
A chance to love, to heal the pain.

Stars align when hearts are true,
With every twist, a chance to find,
The spark that once ignited two,
A map of souls, naturally aligned.

Winding paths bring forth the past,
In laughter shared, in silence deep,
A journey forged, a love that lasts,
In tender vows, our souls we keep.

Together now, we tread as one,
In every step, a promise made,
Through storms and sun, till days are done,
Rediscovery, our hearts' parade.

The Echo of an Old Promise

In twilight's glow, a promise spoke,
In shadows where sweet wishes lay,
An echo weaves through heartstrings' yoke,
Reminds us of the words that sway.

Through laughter's light and whispered fears,
The bond we forged, though weathered now,
In every joy, in every tear,
The vow remains; it will not bow.

As seasons change, the winds still sigh,
Each sigh carries your name with grace,
Like fragile dreams that soar up high,
A dance of time we still embrace.

The candle flickers, soft and bright,
In stillness where old hopes align,
A promise glows in the night,
Everlasting, yours and mine.

A tapestry of years, behold,
In every thread, my heart reflects,
The echo of a promise old,
In every beat, our love connects.

Cradle of Past Emotions

In the cradle of memories, softly lie,
Faded whispers from days of yore,
Each tear a story, each laugh a sigh,
In shadows, we find what we adored.

Cradled gently in time's embrace,
Moments rise and moments fall,
In the tapestry of love's sweet chase,
Each thread a journey, binding all.

Images flicker like stars in dusk,
Reminders of joy, of heart's refrain,
Through scents of spring and autumn's musk,
We find the beauty in the pain.

Time may fray the edges near,
But the core remains, pure and whole,
In that cradle, we hold so dear,
The echoes still nourish our soul.

So let us cherish, embrace the past,
In the cradle where soft love flows,
In every heartbeat, a spell is cast,
Within our hearts, the memory grows.

Whispers of a Blooming Heart

In the garden where dreams softly weave,
Petals unfurl, in their fragrance believe.
The sun spills warmth like a lover's embrace,
Nature's song sings in a sweet, tender space.

With every breeze, secrets begin to sway,
Colors and scents dance in bright array.
A gentle murmur from roots so deep,
Awakens the whispers that hearts long to keep.

Butterflies flutter, they dip and they dart,
A reminder of freedom shared by the heart.
Joy spills forth in each vibrant hue,
In the bloom of a moment, love feels anew.

Time lingers gently, as shadows all bend,
Life's fleeting moments refuse to end.
In every petal, a story unfolds,
Of a heartbeat cherished, a dream it holds.

The night softly wraps the world in its veil,
While stars wink above, like a lover's soft tale.
In this sacred space, where secrets entwine,
A blooming heart whispers, forever is mine.

Echoes of Lost Affection

In the quiet of night, shadows retreat,
Memories linger where two souls did meet.
Whispers of laughter, now fading away,
Time drifts like leaves in a crisp autumn day.

Walls hold the whispers of moments once dear,
Echoing softly, yet painfully clear.
Faded photographs, smiles now seem strange,
Love's gentle shroud wrapped in a heart's change.

Once, fires burned brightly, now embers are cold,
Stories of passion in silence unfold.
Each glance turned away, a reminder too stark,
In echoes of lost affection, we wander in the dark.

Words left unspoken linger in air,
Hopes laid to rest, far beyond our care.
Yet within the void, memories still live,
A testament to love, and all it could give.

Though paths may diverge, and hearts learn to mend,
The echoes of affection may twist and depend.
In the silence that follows, a longing still breathes,
The heart, a quiet hall, where love never leaves.

The Reawakening Touch

A soft brush of fingers, a spark in the night,
Lingers like shadows, drawn into light.
In the hush of the dawn, where dreams intertwine,
Awakening hearts like an intricate vine.

Moments suspended in the warmth of the skin,
Light flickers gently, a dance from within.
Reviving the whispers long buried in dust,
A promise of hope, in touch we can trust.

The world outside fades as we draw near,
Every heartbeat echoes, crystal clear.
Eyes meet like rivers, flowing so free,
In the reawakening touch, just you and me.

Clarity blossoms, as skies turn to blue,
With every heartbeat, old feels like new.
In the tapestry woven of affection and care,
Love's gentle touch whispers, forever we share.

Underneath the stars, with the moon as our guide,
We renew our vow, the heart opens wide.
In this tender moment, souls can entwine,
The reawakening touch, forever divine.

Heartstrings Revived

In the hush of the twilight, shadows proclaim,
The essence of love, like a flickering flame.
Heartstrings entwined, though time pulls apart,
A melody echoes, the song of the heart.

With every new dawn, a chance to reclaim,
The warmth of those moments that called out our names.
In laughter and tears, in silence we float,
Reviving our bond, like a long-forgotten note.

Threads of connection weave in the air,
A tapestry rich, beyond all compare.
Gentle reminders in whispers of fate,
Heartstrings revived, never too late.

Each glance that we share becomes like a spark,
Lighting the path through the shadowy dark.
We find our way back, through storms and through trials,
In the depth of our love, we discover our smiles.

Beyond all the distance and trials we face,
The heart finds its rhythm, a familiar grace.
In the symphony played, our spirits will lift,
Heartstrings once frayed, now a magical gift.

Rebirth in the Shape of Gentle Touches

Whispers soft like morning dew,
Awaken dreams that once were few.
In tender moments, life ignites,
The soul finds peace in warm delights.

Beneath the stars, we find our place,
With every heartbeat, a gentle grace.
New beginnings dance in the air,
A silent promise, love laid bare.

In shadows cast by fading light,
We rise again, ready for flight.
The touch of warmth, the brush of skin,
A testament to where we've been.

Through trials faced and lessons learned,
With every scar, our spirits burned.
Together bound, we take the leap,
In gentle touches, memories keep.

So let the past not weigh us down,
For in this moment, we won't drown.
Rebirth whispers in every sigh,
As gentle touches help us fly.

The Mystery of Hearts Renewed

In silence deep, two souls collide,
Mysteries hidden, love can't hide.
With every glance, a story shared,
Hearts renewed, no longer scared.

The echoes of the past fade slow,
In whispered secrets, feelings grow.
Unraveled threads of fate entwined,
In each new dawn, our hearts aligned.

Beneath the moon, we take our stand,
Each gentle touch, a guiding hand.
With every laugh, we stitch our seams,
The future bright, fulfilled dreams.

Through twists and turns, we find our way,
A dance of joy, we choose to stay.
In unity, our spirits soar,
The mystery lives forevermore.

So here we stand, no fear, just trust,
In love's embrace, it's a must.
Hearts renewed, we face the night,
With every heartbeat, purest light.

Stars Aligned for a Second Embrace

In twilight's glow, the stars conspire,
To guide our hearts through endless fire.
Twinkling whispers in the dark,
A second chance ignites the spark.

With open arms, we greet the dawn,
The magic of the night not gone.
In every sigh, the world feels right,
Stars aligned beneath the night.

Electric dreams dance in our eyes,
Rekindled love beneath gray skies.
In cosmic rhythms, we entwine,
Two beating hearts, a love divine.

Each moment shared, a perfect grace,
In every touch, we find our place.
The universe conspired so,
To cradle us, forever glow.

Through time and space, we've faced the tide,
In our embrace, we both confide.
With stars aligned, we'll always be,
In love's embrace, eternally free.

A Journey Back to Where We Began

With every step, the echoes call,
Back to the place where love stood tall.
A winding path of joy and pain,
We trace the lines, our hearts remain.

In laughter shared, in tears we spilled,\nThe memories
formed, the voids fulfilled.
Through tangled roads, we find our way,
In every moment, night and day.

The sun will rise on dreams once lost,
Together still, no matter the cost.
A journey back, hand in hand,
To where we breathe, to where we stand.

Through gentle whispers in the breeze,
Our souls entwined, forever pleased.
In sacred spaces, we renew,
The promise held, forever true.

So here we are, back to the start,
With open arms and open heart.
A journey back, where love unfolds,
In stories shared, our truth retold.

A Revival of Heartbeats

In the stillness where dreams reside,
Hope whispers softly, drawing near.
Morning light breaks through the night,
Painting shadows with shades of cheer.

Old wounds heal in the warmth of dawn,
Life pulses anew and dreams take flight.
Every heartbeat sings a song,
A melody that feels just right.

In the silence, love finds its voice,
Embracing the moments lost in time.
A revival blooms with every choice,
As hearts entwine in rhythm and rhyme.

With every breath, we forge anew,
A tapestry of life we weave.
With courage, we greet the morning dew,
Knowing together, we can believe.

So let us dance with open hearts,
In the symphony of a brand new start.
For in this space where love imparts,
A revival of beat, a fresh work of art.

Illuminating Forgotten Places

In corners where shadows used to loom,
Light floods in, casting warmth anew.
Forgotten paths begin to bloom,
Emerging hope in every hue.

Whispers echo through the trees,
Memories linger in soft embrace.
The world awakens with gentle ease,
Illuminating a once-hidden place.

Faded photographs, stories unfold,
With every glimmer, history speaks.
A tapestry of dreams retold,
In every heart, a longing peaks.

With open eyes, we seek and find,
The beauty in what time obscured.
Each moment brings a chance combined,
To cherish all that now feels assured.

So let our hearts be guides through time,
In spaces once lost, let love ignite.
For in each whisper, we can climb,
Illuminating the darkest night.

Whispers of the Heart's Awakening

Gentle breezes carry sweet sighs,
Rustling leaves that dance above.
A symphony of soft replies,
Awakening the pulse of love.

In silence, truths begin to stir,
From depths long buried, hopes arise.
Every heartbeat sings a blur,
A melody, a sweet surprise.

With every dawn, we start anew,
Embracing all the light can bring.
A canvas fresh, a vibrant hue,
Of whispers that our spirits sing.

As petals open, dewdrops gleam,
With every touch, our souls align.
In the hushed moments, we redeem,
The quiet notes of love divine.

So let the whispers guide our way,
In journeys where our hearts can play.
For in each echo, bright and gay,
Awakening, we find our stay.

Echoes of Forgotten Affections

In long-lost letters, ink once bled,
Secrets shared beneath the moon.
Each written word a promise said,
In echoes that still hum the tune.

Time has woven threads of fate,
Yet love's soft call still lingers here.
With every memory, we await,
The touch of hearts that once were near.

Fading photographs tell their tales,
Of laughter, tears, and sweet regret.
In every glance, a hope prevails,
Echoes of love we won't forget.

As seasons change, the heart still yearns,
For all the moments that we took.
In every whisper, the spirit burns,
A testament in each old book.

So let us cherish what remains,
The echoes of affection true.
For in our hearts, love never wanes,
It pulses on, forever new.

A Journey Back to Radiance

Under the shadows, hope does gleam,
Whispers of light in the silent stream.
With every step, the heart does race,
Seeking the warmth of a sunlit place.

Through valleys deep, and mountains high,
The spirit soars, like a bird in the sky.
Each moment a path, each breath a guide,
In the embrace of love, we shall abide.

The stars align, guiding our way,
Through darkened nights, we find our sway.
With courage strong, we face the dawn,
Embracing the light, as fears are gone.

The journey unfolds, a tapestry spun,
Threads of gold woven, we are one.
In the treasure of time, memories bright,
We dance in the glow of the endless light.

A journey complete, yet never ends,
For in the heart, the light transcends.
Back to radiance, where dreams ignite,
Together we shine, forever in flight.

The Return of Starlit Dreams

In twilight's grasp, where dreams reside,
The stars awaken, their arms open wide.
A gentle breeze whispers their names,
Calling us forth to play their games.

Once lost in shadows, hopes now bright,
Guided by the soft, celestial light.
A canvas vast, where wishes take flight,
In the quiet night, all feels right.

Chasing the echoes of distant stars,
We dance through galaxies, healing scars.
Each spark a memory, a wish fulfilled,\nIn the cosmic
rhythm, our spirits thrilled.

The moonlight wraps us, a silken thread,
We wander through realms where fears have fled.
In this return, we find our way,
To starlit dreams where we gladly stay.

As dawn draws near, the stars say goodbye,
Yet in our hearts, their light will not die.
We carry their magic, as we awake,
In the day's embrace, our dreams won't shake.

The Dance of Two Souls

In the stillness, a rhythm begins,
Two souls entwined, where love never thins.
With every glance, the world fades away,
In the dance of hearts, we softly sway.

Whispers of laughter, a song in the breeze,
Drawn to each other with effortless ease.
In harmony's embrace, we find our place,
In the warmth of joy, we touch grace.

The stars spin around as we move in time,
Every heartbeat a pulse, a sweet rhyme.
Together we journey through night and day,
In the dance of life, we boldly play.

With hands held tight, we leap and twirl,
Lost in the magic of love's sweet swirl.
No fear of tomorrow, just this timeless bliss,
In the dance of two souls, we find our kiss.

As the music fades, the silence speaks,
In perfect balance, our love just peaks.
Forever we'll dance, in light and in shade,
In the rhythm of life, love will never fade.

Sunlight After the Storm

After the tempest, the world stands still,
Hope rises anew, with a gentle thrill.
Tears of the sky wash the earth so pure,
In the aftermath, we will endure.

Emerging from shadows, we glimpse the light,
A golden promise, breaking the night.
With every ray, a warmth ignites,
In the embrace of dawn, the heart unites.

The storm may rage, but we find our way,
Through trials faced, we learn to stay.
In the vibrant flowers, a story unfolds,
Of resilience cherished, as each one holds.

As sunlight dances on glistening dew,
We rise from the depths, born anew.
From challenges faced, our spirits soar,
Together we stand, stronger than before.

In the harmony of life, we find our song,
In valleys and peaks, where we belong.
With hearts illuminated, we greet each new norm,
In the brilliance of life, we weather the storm.

Renewal Beneath the Stars

Under the vast night sky, we stand,
Whispers of dreams borne by the breeze.
Each twinkle, a promise, a helping hand,
In the stillness, our worries cease.

The world feels light, the heart aglow,
With constellations mapping our fate.
In the silence, we find room to grow,
Every moment, love finds its rate.

Hope unfolds like a flower in spring,
While shadows retreat, and light takes hold.
In the universe, our spirits sing,
A renewal in stories untold.

Together we cast away old fears,
As time dances softly around us.
In the laughter, we shed past tears,
In this moment, it's just us.

So beneath the stars, our dreams ignite,
A canvas of wishes painted anew.
With the universe wrapped in this night,
We find home in the warmth of you.

The Bridge Back to You

Across the river of time we've sailed,
With currents that pulled us apart.
But in every storm, love prevailed,
Drawing maps back to the heart.

Each step I take, a stone laid down,
On a bridge forged from memories strong.
No distance can wear away this crown,
For in your arms, I belong.

Through whispered paths of the past we tread,
The echoes of laughter linger still.
With every heartbeat, our colors spread,
Painting futures we dare to fulfill.

With hope as our compass guiding true,
I'll traverse the shadows of doubt.
For the bridge I seek leads back to you,
A love I will never live without.

So hand in hand, let's embrace the light,
Together, we'll conquer the unknown.
In your eyes, I see the night,
And find my way back home.

Reverberations of Untold Stories

In the silence, stories whisper low,
Echoes of lives lived, lessons learned.
With every heartbeat, past seeds we sow,
In the dusk, their wisdom returned.

Time carries tales woven in gold,
In shadows cast by laughter and pain.
Every moment, a new truth unfolds,
With the sunrise, we rise again.

Across the ages, spirits entwined,
Writing their chapters in stars above.
Every heartbeat, a thread to remind,
Of the power of memory and love.

Let us gather these fragments and share,
Each verse a glimpse into the soul.
Together, we breathe this vibrant air,
And in unity, we become whole.

So listen closely to the voices of yore,
In their echoes, we find who we are.
For the past is a gift we can't ignore,
Reverberations of stories, our guiding star.

Chasing Fragments of Us

In the quiet hours of fading light,
I search for traces of what we've shared.
Through the mist, shadows take their flight,
Fragments of us, forever ensnared.

Each memory a petal in the wind,
Scattered across paths we used to roam.
In the heart where love has always been,
I gather pieces, stitch them to home.

With every glance, the past reflects clear,
In laughter, in tears, we find our way.
Through the echoes of joy and of fear,
I chase the remnants of yesterday.

To a future where dreams are reborn,
Where echoes of love guide our flight.
In the beauty of dusk, hope is worn,
As stars beckon with their soft light.

So in the chase, I feel you near,
In every corner, your essence thrives.
Together, through love, we conquer fear,
Chasing fragments, where true life derives.

Veils of Emotions Lifted

Behind the veil, a whisper lies,
Hidden truths in shadowed sighs.
Hearts awaken, softly glow,
Veils of emotions begin to flow.

A gentle touch, a fleeting smile,
Promises linger for a while.
Beneath the surface, feelings wake,
The silent bond we yearn to make.

In the silence, echoes soar,
Connecting souls forevermore.
Layers shed, we stand revealed,
In the light, our doubts concealed.

Time dances on, the moments shared,
In tender hands, our hearts bared.
Veils lifted, visions clear,
Emotions rise, no room for fear.

Together we forge a brand new way,
In every breath, in every sway.
Veils of emotions, we embrace,
A journey shared, a sacred space.

A Pathway Paved in Memories

Along the pathway, shadows play,
Cobblestones where we'd once stay.
Each step echoes a laugh we shared,
In the whispers, memories cared.

Sunset hues on autumn leaves,
Tales of love our heart believes.
A tapestry of cherished days,
In time's embrace, our spirit stays.

Old photographs, a fleeting glance,
In every look, a second chance.
Gathered moments, stitched in gold,
A future bright, as stories unfold.

Under stars, we walked as one,
Traced our dreams till night was done.
A path we paved with joy and grace,
In every turn, love's warm trace.

As seasons shift, we'll wander near,
In laughter's ring and silent cheer.
This pathway calls us home to be,
In memories, we're forever free.

Awakened Embraces

In dawn's light, we find our way,
Awakened hearts, come what may.
A gentle hug, a soft caress,
In warm embraces, we find rest.

With every sunrise, hope renewed,
Together, we crush solitude.
Fingers entwined, like roots of trees,
In love's embrace, we find our ease.

The silent language of a glance,
In every moment, love's sweet dance.
Together we breathe, our spirits blend,
In awakened joy, we transcend.

Through trials faced and storms we ride,
In each embrace, we confide.
Together stronger, come what may,
Awakened hearts, we find our way.

As twilight whispers, day's embrace,
In stillness found, a sacred space.
With open arms, we welcome night,
Awakened embraces hold us tight.

A Serenade to the Stars

Beneath the sky, where dreams ignite,
We sing a serenade at night.
Stars above our guiding lights,
In melody, our hearts take flight.

Each twinkle holds a story dear,
Whispers soft, the cosmos near.
In constellations, secrets shared,
A serenade of love declared.

Moonlit paths, we boldly tread,
With every note, our spirits fed.
Awake in wonder, lost in glow,
To the stars, our voices flow.

In harmony, we find delight,
Through every shadow, every night.
A cosmic dance, a timeless rhyme,
Our serenade defies all time.

So let the heavens listen well,
To every wish and dream we tell.
With hearts ablaze, we seek the night,
In a serenade, we take our flight.

A Symphony of Second Chances

In echoes soft, a melody plays,
Life's notes entwined in tangled arrays.
With each dawn's light, hope finds its way,
A chance to begin, a brand new day.

Mistakes once made, now fade from the mind,
New paths to tread, we leave woes behind.
In harmony's grace, we search and align,
A symphony grows, our hearts will entwine.

Every stumble leads to a dance anew,
In vibrant hues where the old meets the new.
We rise from the shadows, embrace the bright view,
With courage as music, we'll find what is true.

From ashes we spring, like blossoms in spring,
With petals unfurling, our voices will sing.
The notes of our journey, forever they cling,
A symphony pulses, a radiant ring.

So let us rejoice, for all we have learned,
In the fires of trials, our spirits have burned.
With each beat of life, new chapters are turned,
A symphony sweetly, our hearts have discerned.

Embrace of Forgotten Flames

In twilight's glow, memories stir,
Whispers of warmth, long lost to the blur.
Flames that once flickered, now softly gleam,
In shadows of silence, we kindle the dream.

These embers of passion, once flickered so bright,
A dance of the past, now ignited by light.
Together we wander, where shadows retreat,
Embrace of the flames, in rhythm we meet.

Tenderly forged in the crucible's fire,
Desires rekindled in softened choir.
Lost in the echoes, where time dares to bend,
Forgotten yet cherished, we rise and ascend.

Through corridors of longing, our spirits ignite,
In the tapestry woven, love's thread shines so bright.
Passion awakens, as hearts re-align,
In embrace of forgotten, our souls redefine.

So let the flames burn, a beacon of trust,
In warmth and in whispers, we feel we must.
An embrace of the past, revitalized grace,
In flames that were forgotten, we find our own place.

The Pulse of New Beginnings

A heartbeat whispers, the dawn of a day,
With every breath, we chase shadows away.
In moments of stillness, the future unfolds,
A pulse of new life, in stories retold.

Each step we take, a fresh note to compose,
In the garden of dreams where possibility grows.
The canvas awaits with colors so bright,
We paint our tomorrows with hope and with light.

In the rustle of leaves, a promise is found,
In the laughter of children, our spirits are crowned.
Together we thrive, in the warmth of the sun,
The pulse of new beginnings has only begun.

With courage as compass, we chart our own way,
As shadows grow long, we greet the new day.
The rhythm of life, a symphony bold,
In the pulse of new beginnings, our stories unfold.

So let us dance wildly, with hearts open wide,
Embracing the changes, with love as our guide.
The pulse of new beginnings, it sings in our soul,
In this journey of life, we find ourselves whole.

Breaths of Reunited Souls

In softest whispers, our paths intertwine,
With breaths in sync, your heart beats with mine.
Across time and space, our spirits have soared,
In breaths of reunion, sweet love is restored.

Through seasons of absence, we searched for the spark,
In shadows of longing, igniting the dark.
The magic of destiny, bringing us near,
In breaths of united, our vision is clear.

With gazes like fires, we light up the night,
In the dance of our souls, everything feels right.
Together we blossom, like flowers in bloom,
In breaths of connection, dispelling all gloom.

Each heartbeat resounds, a symphony vast,
In the melody woven, our love unsurpassed.
In moments embraced, where time holds its breath,
The breaths of reunited, a victory over death.

So take my hand, dear, let's traverse this whole,
In the breaths of our journey, we find our true role.
Together forever, through joy and through strife,
In breaths of united souls, we celebrate life.

Embracing the Softness of Spring

Petals drift upon the breeze,
Colors bloom beneath the trees.
Whispers of a gentle rain,
Nature sings its sweet refrain.

Morning light begins to glow,
Warming hearts in tender flow.
Chirping birds in joyous flight,
Bring the promise of delight.

Laughter echoes in the air,
Joyful moments, free of care.
Every bud a story told,
In the sunlight, bright and bold.

As we walk through fields of green,
Hand in hand, a lovely scene.
With each step, we share a dream,
In this gentle, soothing theme.

Embracing springs, we dance and sway,
Life awakens in this play.
Tender moments intertwined,
Love's soft echo, refined.

The Return of Gentle Radiance

Sunlight breaks the silent night,
Softly bringing back the light.
Shadows fade and fears retreat,
Life renews with rhythmic beat.

Gentle rays caress the ground,
In their warmth, a joy is found.
Colors paint the waking skies,
In their glow, our spirits rise.

Fingers trace the morning dew,
Moments cherished, ever new.
Every glance, a spark divine,
Light returns, and hearts align.

Whispers dance upon the air,
Hope and love, beyond compare.
With each ray, we start to mend,
Gentle radiance, our friend.

In this dawn, we find our way,
Guided by the sun's warm ray.
Through the clouds, the bright begins,
A new journey here begins.

Threads of Passion Intertwined Again

In the weave of tender touch,
Each thread speaks of love so much.
Hearts embrace in silent grace,
Filling every empty space.

Moments linger, time stands still,
Every heartbeat shows the thrill.
Through the night, a dance we share,
Wrapped in dreams beyond compare.

Every glance, a spark ignites,
Passion's flame, a pure delight.
In the quiet, whispers flow,
A tapestry of love will grow.

Underneath the stars we lay,
Bound together, night and day.
Threads of fate, so finely spun,
A journey shared, forever begun.

In each moment, find the thrill,
With every touch, the hearts fulfill.
Together strong, we shall remain,
Threads of passion, intertwined again.

Sunrise over Winter's Remnants

Golden rays break through the frost,
Winter's hold, forever lost.
Silent whispers sigh goodbye,
As the bluebirds start to fly.

Fields adorned in melting white,
Transformation feels so right.
Nature wakes, the world reborn,
In the glow of early morn.

Every shadow slowly fades,
Giving way to bright cascades.
Hope emerges from the cold,
Stories of the brave retold.

Sunrise paints the sky anew,
With each hue, our dreams imbue.
In every heartbeat, life begins,
Winter's tale now softly thins.

As we walk through glistening dew,
Past blooms promise, ever true.
Sunshine whispers, "Time to rise,"
As we reach for bluer skies.

A Serenade to Growing Affection

In the quiet of the night,
Whispers weave like threads of gold,
Hearts entwined in gentle light,
Emotions bloom, a story told.

Each glance a promise softly made,
Hands that touch and pause to feel,
In every serenade displayed,
Love's sweet dance, a tender reel.

With every laugh, a note takes flight,
Melodies of joy we share,
In shadows cast by silvered light,
We find a world beyond compare.

As seasons change, so do we grow,
Roots of trust run deep and wide,
Through storms and sun, love's constant glow,
Together, walking side by side.

In each soft sigh, a bond expands,
Together we compose our song,
A serenade in tender hands,
Growing ever deep and strong.

Timber of Time

Old trees whisper tales of yore,
Roots reach deep, in earth they bind,
Lives entwined, forevermore,
Weathered yet true, their strength defined.

Branches stretch, as dreams take flight,
Leaves that dance in summer's breeze,
Within their shade, all feels right,
Bearing witness to time's decrees.

Seasons pass in a quiet flow,
Letting go, embracing change,
Stories etched in bark like snow,
A dance of life, steadfast and strange.

Through the storms, they bow and bend,
Yet rise again, with roots held tight,
An ageless strength that will not end,
In the heart of day and night.

Timber of time, a saga stands,
Enduring love, its legacy,
Each ring a circle, fate commands,
In nature's arms, we find our glee.

Weathered Yet Strong

The winds have worn my edges thin,
Tales of trials molded my face,
Yet through the storms, I found my kin,
Embracing life with calm embrace.

Fallen leaves that danced my path,
Speak of seasons, both joy and pain,
In laughter's light, I find no wrath,
For every drop brings growth, not bane.

A tapestry of scars I wear,
Each mark a testament to the fight,
Weathered yet strong beyond compare,
In shadows cast, I find the light.

With every storm, a chance to grow,
Roots plunge deeper, hearts take flight,
In resilience, love tends to sow,
A garden blooming, pure delight.

For there is beauty in the worn,
A story whispered on the breeze,
Weathered yet strong, my heart reborn,
In every challenge, I find peace.

Fragments of Us Under the Same Sky

Underneath the endless blue,
Starry nights call out our name,
Sparkling dreams in every hue,
Fragments of us, a timeless flame.

Across the miles, hearts beat as one,
Moments captured like fleeting light,
In the embrace of setting sun,
We weave our dreams into the night.

Words unspoken, a language shared,
In glances bright, the world stands still,
Each echo soft, each glance declared,
A dance of love, a cosmic thrill.

Though distances may stretch and pull,
Beneath the same sky, we remain,
In every heartbeat, every lull,
Fragments of us cannot wane.

For love, like stars, forever shines,
Guiding paths through darkened days,
In every twinkle, it aligns,
Fragments of us in endless ways.

The Reawakening of Silent Yearnings

In the stillness of the dawn,
Whispers float like morning air,
Silent yearnings, dreams reborn,
A hopeful heart begins to dare.

Gentle rays caress the ground,
Awakening the dust of time,
In this moment, peace is found,
Yearnings hum a sacred rhyme.

Through shadows past, a light breaks through,
Each heartbeat sings a brand new song,
The world alive, a vibrant hue,
Silent yearnings, no more wrong.

As petals bloom and spirits rise,
Transforming grief into pure grace,
A tapestry of love, no lies,
Reawakening in life's embrace.

In every dawn, a chance to see,
The beauty in each silent plea,
Yearnings bloom, wild and free,
A symphony of you and me.

Whispers on the Wind

In the hush of twilight glow,
Soft secrets float and flow.
Rustling leaves, a gentle breeze,
Carrying thoughts with such ease.

Echoes dance beneath the stars,
Tales of love from near and far.
Every sigh, a fleeting rhyme,
Lost in the arms of time.

Whispers speak of days long gone,
Fleeting moments, dusk to dawn.
Nature's breath, a sweet embrace,
Holding dreams in sacred space.

Through the night, the stories glide,
Softening the heart's great tide.
Night's embrace, a tender sigh,
In the silence, spirits fly.

In each gust, a wish is spun,
Carried forth, where rivers run.
Whispers weave a tapestry,
Of love and hope, eternally.

A Song for Forgotten Hearts

Once a time, love's sweet refrain,
Faded echoes, joy and pain.
Silent dreams start to depart,
Leaving shadows on the heart.

In the dim light, memories play,
Dancing softly, gone astray.
Every note, a tear uncried,
A haunting tune where hopes reside.

Forgotten tales of laughter's song,
Lingering where hearts belong.
Soft melodies of days gone past,
Whispering love that couldn't last.

In the twilight, voices blend,
Yearning dreams that never end.
A song for hearts that time forgot,
Melodies in shadows caught.

Through the night, the echoes creep,
In the silence, secrets keep.
A harmony of lost delight,
Resonating through the night.

Fragments of Once-Lost Dreams

Scattered pieces on the floor,
Whispers of what was before.
In the dust, a shadow's trace,
Memories that time can't erase.

Glimmers of a distant song,
Where the heart would feel so strong.
Each fragment tells a story true,
Of all the hopes that once we knew.

In the silence of the night,
Dreams emerge to share their light.
Tender visions start to weave,
Promises that we believe.

Lost in rapture, hopes abide,
In the pieces, love's great tide.
Every dream, a whispered call,
In their beauty, we stand tall.

Through the cracks, a light will gleam,
Rekindling once-lost dreams.
With each shard, a path is found,
In the silence, love resounds.

Resilient Roses in December

Snowflakes fall, the world turns white,
In the cold, a hidden light.
Amidst the frost, a rose will bloom,
Defying winter's icy gloom.

Petals bright against the grey,
Whispers of a brighter day.
Strength in beauty, grace bestowed,
In the harsh, the heart's abode.

Through the chill, the colors rise,
Revealing warmth beneath the skies.
Each thorn, a story of its own,
A testament to seeds once sown.

In quiet strength, the blossoms sway,
Finding warmth in winter's fray.
Resilient spirits, bold and free,
Roses teach us how to be.

Hope unfurls, fierce and bright,
Blooming soft in the fading light.
Through the cold, they find their place,
In December's warm embrace.

The Blooming of Old Desires

Petals unfurl with gentle sighs,
Whispers of dreams from long ago.
In twilight's soft, embracing light,
Forgotten hopes begin to glow.

Silent echoes of laughter chase,
Faded echoes in the breeze.
Hearts that waited, clocked in space,
Now entwined, finding their ease.

Time, the gardener of our souls,
Watering roots beneath the ground.
Old desires in vibrant roles,
In fragrant blooms, love's spell is found.

With every breeze, a promise stirs,
Reviving tales that once were told.
As life composes its sweet verse,
We dance anew, so brave and bold.

In this garden of love's rebirth,
Seeds of passion, tenderly sown.
A flourishing fire, beyond worth,
Creating a world of our own.

Rekindled Flames in Autumn's Embrace

Leaves turn gold in bitter chill,
Nature whispers of the past.
With every breeze, hearts softly thrill,
As warmth returns, a spell is cast.

Bonfire crackles, sparks arise,
In shadows dance the lost and found.
Between the sighs and longing cries,
Old flames dance with a familiar sound.

Scarves wrapped tight against the night,
We speak of dreams unspoken, rare.
In autumn's breath, there's pure delight,
As old wounds mend, we breathe the air.

Moments linger, time stands still,
With every glance, passions ignite.
In shared laughter, our hearts fulfill,
Two souls united in golden light.

With every leaf, a story told,
Of rekindled love, fierce and bright.
In longing's grasp, we bravely hold,
As autumn wraps us in its night.

Heartstrings Rewoven in Moonlight

Beneath the silvered, gleaming sky,
We weave our tales of dream and hope.
In whispered secrets, truths gone by,
Our hearts entwined, we learn to cope.

Moonlight dances on the ground,
Casting shadows bold and deep.
In quiet tones, love can be found,
As promises begin to seep.

Threads of warmth, a loving hand,
Reforming bonds once frayed at ends.
In night's embrace, we take our stand,
With every heartbeat, love transcends.

Stars above, our silent guides,
In cosmic wonders, we confide.
The night reveals where hope resides,
As heartstrings bind, we cannot hide.

Here under heavens vast and wide,
We weave our dreams like silken thread.
In moonlight's glow, fate won't divide,
For love shall flourish, fierce and spread.

A Dance Beneath Revived Stars

In twilight's arms, we find our place,
As stars awaken in the night.
With every step, we slow our pace,
Embracing all that feels so right.

Lost in rhythm, hearts align,
With the universe as our guide.
In every twirl, your eyes shine,
Under cosmos, love's true pride.

Galaxies swirl in our embrace,
While dreams align, we take to flight.
In every movement, pure grace,
The cosmos spins in ethereal light.

Through shadows deep, we glide and sway,
With laughter carried on the wind.
In this eternal, joyful play,
Together, we have found our kin.

With every star, a wish we cast,
For love eternal to explore.
In dances slow, our hearts are vast,
Beneath revived stars, we want for more.

Unraveled Hearts in the Twilight Glow

In twilight's grace, we slowly part,
The shadows dance, revealing art.
Whispers of love, soft and slight,
Unraveled hearts in fading light.

A gentle breeze through fading trees,
Sings lullabies of distant seas.
Promises lost, in silence stow,
Yearning souls in twilight glow.

The secrets shared beneath the stars,
Echo through night, near and far.
In each glance, a story flows,
Unraveled hearts, where sorrow goes.

Yet hope ignites within our core,
As night unveils a brighter shore.
We mend the seams that came undone,
Together rise, two hearts as one.

In twilight's hold, we find our way,
Love's tapestry, woven each day.
From shadows deep, to joy we grow,
Unraveled hearts in twilight's glow.

When Shadows Fade and Joy Returns

When shadows fade, the dawn breaks clear,
Awakening life, drawing near.
Whispers of hope in the morning light,
Chasing away the lingering night.

In gardens where laughter used to bloom,
Through walls of silence, we pierce the gloom.
With every step, new dreams arise,
When shadows fade, we touch the skies.

The song of the heart begins to play,
A melody sweet, a brand new day.
With every tear, a lesson learned,
When shadows fade, the fire returns.

Embracing the warmth of the sun's embrace,
Finding the light in a sacred space.
Together we rise, hand in hand we yearn,
When shadows fade, our spirits burn.

In the soft glow where hope prevails,
We cast away fears and broken trails.
With laughter and joy, the world we'll turn,
When shadows fade, and joy returns.

The Rebirth of Distant Dreams

In the silence of night, a soft refrain,
Distant dreams stir from slumber's chain.
They rise like stars, scattered and bright,
Whispers of hope in the velvet night.

Once lost in the echoes of time and space,
Now finding their voice in a sacred place.
With every heartbeat, their essence streams,
Embracing the rebirth of distant dreams.

Through shadows that linger and fears that bind,
We chase the light, leaving darkness behind.
The world awakens with colors anew,
The rebirth of dreams, a vibrant view.

Each tear that fell paved the path we tread,
Filling the canvas with stories unsaid.
With courage ignited, we bridge the seams,
In harmony echoing the distant dreams.

Brighter horizons beckon with grace,
Carrying visions, our souls embrace.
Together we soar, beyond what redeems,
Embracing the beauty of distant dreams.

Sunlit Paths to Heart's Renewal

On sunlit paths where petals lay,
We wander softly, come what may.
A healing breeze to gently guide,
To heart's renewal, side by side.

In gardens rich with laughter's tune,
Beneath the watch of a radiant moon.
We shed our fears, let worries go,
On sunlit paths, our spirits grow.

Each step we take, a promise made,
In vibrant hues, our worries fade.
With every dawn, new love ignites,
Sunlit paths to joyful heights.

Through tangled thorns and shadows' flight,
We find our way into the light.
A tapestry of dreams unfurls,
As sunlit paths bring hope to worlds.

In every heartbeat, a whisper flows,
Telling tales that the heart knows.
To cherish the journey and the view,
On sunlit paths, our hearts renew.

In the Garden of Recollection

Among the blooms, memories weave,
Whispers of laughter, shadows that leave.
Time stands still in the softest light,
Petals fall gently, a sweet delight.

Winding paths of old, I tread,
Each step a story, lovingly spread.
Nature's embrace, a tender sigh,
In this garden, love cannot die.

Sunlight dances on leaves so green,
In this haven, solace is seen.
Echoes of voices, sweet and clear,
In the garden, we find what we hold dear.

Every flower holds a piece of past,
Promises whispered, forever to last.
In the hush, a comfort so wide,
In this garden, memories abide.

With every season, changes unfold,
Stories of hearts, brave and bold.
In the twilight, as shadows blend,
In this garden, love transcends.

Healing in Familiar Hands

In the warmth of dawn's embrace,
Healing finds a gentle place.
Familiar hands, a soft caress,
In their touch, I find my rest.

Each bruise and scar, a tale to tell,
In their grasp, I slowly dwell.
Words unspoken, softly shared,
In this moment, I feel cared.

Time slows down, the world asked to wait,
Together we mend, it feels so straight.
Trust entwined in every glance,
In healing hands, we take a chance.

Wounds unfurl with tender grace,
In this haven, we find our space.
Breaths entwined in the morning air,
In familiar hands, we'll repair.

With every touch, I start to bloom,
In the safety, I shed my gloom.
Together we stand, strong and free,
In healing hands, just you and me.

Cultivating Hearts Once More

In the soil of shared dreams,
Hope sprouts forth in vibrant beams.
With every seed, a promise sown,
In cultivating hearts, love is grown.

Tending to the roots, we stand,
Together we nurture, hand in hand.
Through seasons' change, we learn and thrive,
In this garden, we feel alive.

Clouds may gather, storms may roar,
Yet in our hearts, we seek for more.
Light breaks through, a radiant glow,
In cultivated hearts, warmth will flow.

Patience blooms, in silence heard,
In the stillness, every word.
Showers of joy rain down like song,
In cultivating hearts, we belong.

With love as our guide, we journey on,
In this unity, we're never alone.
Crafting a future, strong and pure,
In cultivating hearts, we endure.

Petals of Passion Reopened

With every dawn, new petals curl,
Whispers of passion begin to twirl.
Colors burst in the morning hue,
In tenderness, we find what's true.

Resilience blooms where shadows lay,
In scars of love, we find our way.
Gentle sighs in the evening's glow,
In petals of passion, feelings grow.

Time reassures with a soft embrace,
In the heart, there's a sacred space.
Hearts unfold in a rhythmic dance,
In passion's light, we take a chance.

Every touch, a spark ignites,
In this garden, endless delights.
With open hearts, we dare to dream,
In petals of passion, love's supreme.

Every moment, a treasure to hold,
In stories of love, we dare to be bold.
With every heartbeat, feelings soar,
In petals of passion, forevermore.

A Canvas of Tender Revisions

Brushstrokes mix in colors bright,
Pastels whisper in the light.
Each layer tells a tale anew,
Of moments wrapped in gentle hue.

Framed in joy, framed in pain,
Memories like soft refrains.
They shift and sway with every glance,
Inviting us to take a chance.

On this canvas, dreams reside,
Hopes and fears, they step outside.
In the blend of dusk and dawn,
Each sigh and smile lingers on.

With every touch, the story grows,
In shades of love, it beautifully flows.
Revisions made, yet true to heart,
A masterpiece, a work of art.

Tender moments, strokes of bliss,
In the silence, find a kiss.
A journey defined by every hue,
In this canvas, we begin anew.

The Dance of Old Hopes

Beneath the stars, old dreams collide,
In whispered tales, they do confide.
Shadows twirl with laughter's ring,
As echoes of the past take wing.

In moonlit nights, we find our way,
To where the heart had longed to stay.
Twilight's grace, a partner's glance,
Reviving each forgotten dance.

With every step, the heart ignites,
A melody of sweet delights.
Faded hopes like flowers bloom,
In every corner of the room.

Holding on to whispers past,
In this dance, we find our cast.
Old hopes flicker in the light,
Guiding us through the night.

Together in this fleeting trance,
We sway in time, a waltzing chance.
The dance of old hopes, bold and true,
Leads us back to me and you.

Shadows of Longing Revisited

In the dusk, shadows linger near,
Whispering secrets we hold dear.
With every breath, the past unfolds,
Tales of hearts and love retold.

Longing calls in silent tones,
Through the cracks of ancient stones.
Memories dance like falling leaves,
Wrapped in the night, the heart believes.

Fragments drift like stories spun,
In twilight's glow, the journey's begun.
Each shadow holds a longing glance,
A silent sigh, a hopeful chance.

With every flash of recent dreams,
In endless night, a longing gleams.
These shadows cast, both soft and light,
Revisit dreams that take to flight.

As we wander through the haze,
Longing's song in gentle praise.
Shadows weave a tapestry,
Of what was, and what could be.

Seasons of Abiding Passion

In spring, the blooms of love emerge,
Each petal whispers, hearts converge.
Beneath the sun, wildflowers rise,
In every glance, a sweet surprise.

Summer brings the sultry days,
Passion's fire in golden rays.
Underneath the starlit skies,
Desires dance, and spirit flies.

Autumn's hues, a rich embrace,
Leaves cascading, a tender grace.
In silence shared, we find our way,
With every rustle, love will stay.

Winter's chill cannot contain,
The warmth we feel, the joy, the pain.
In cozy corners, dreams take flight,
Igniting hearts through frosty nights.

Through seasons change, our love remains,
An enduring bond that love sustains.
In every moment, passion grows,
Through life's embrace, the heart just knows.

The Silence Between One Another

In the hush of evening's glow,
Words unspoken softly flow.
Between us lies a gentle space,
Where silence wears a tender face.

Eyes meet, yet voices fade,
In this quiet serenade.
The weight of longing hangs so close,
In silence, love reveals the most.

Each heartbeat echoes through the night,
A rhythm lost, but feeling right.
In this moment, time stands still,
A fragile bond we both can feel.

We are two stars in twilight's seam,
Bound by a shared, unbroken dream.
In the silence, we learn to trust,
As whispers fade, it's love that's just.

So let the stillness speak its song,
In the quiet, we both belong.
With every breath, the silence grows,
Between us, love, the answer shows.

Flickers of Familiar Warmth

In cozy corners, shadows play,
Flickers dance, brightening the day.
Remnants of laughter fill the air,
In shared memories, we linger there.

A touch of hand, the softest brush,
In familiar warmth, we feel the rush.
Echoes of joy in every sigh,
A spark ignites, we learn to fly.

The world outside fades from our view,
In this haven, it's me and you.
The fire crackles, the shadows swirl,
Flickers of warmth, like a precious pearl.

We weave our stories, thread by thread,
In whispered tones, our hearts are led.
In this embrace, time slips away,
Together, forever, in soft array.

So let the flickers guide our way,
In warmth, we find what words can't say.
Hand in hand, through night and morn,
In familiar glow, our love is born.

Rediscovering the Twinkle in Your Eye

Once more, I see the spark ignite,
The twinkle in your eye, so bright.
It dances there like morning dew,
A whisper of love, tried and true.

Through seasons past, the shadows played,
Yet in your gaze, my heart regained.
A glimmer shines, the past draws near,
In your smile, I lose my fear.

Moments woven with threads of light,
Each glance a promise, burning bright.
In laughter shared, our spirits rise,
Together we reach for the skies.

The twinkle speaks of stories old,
Of dreams alive, yet to unfold.
In every look, our love resides,
Rediscovering the joy inside.

So let this spark eternally glow,
A beacon for the paths we'll go.
In every twilight, every morn,
The twinkle in your eye, reborn.

Tides of Emotion Restored

The ocean's breath, a soothing balm,
Waves crash gently, bringing calm.
Tides of love, forever flow,
In rhythm with the heart's deep glow.

Each movement tells a tale anew,
Of moments shared, just me and you.
In ebb and flow, we find our pace,
The tides of time embrace our grace.

Through stormy nights and golden sun,
Together we rise, united as one.
The ocean sings of love's decree,
In each wave, our spirits free.

With every tide, emotions shift,
Yet in the deep, our hearts uplift.
The salty air, a whispered cheer,
In every tide, I hold you near.

So let the waters guide our way,
With every rise and fall, we sway.
In tides of love, we're forever bound,
In the ocean's arms, our peace is found.

Warmth Under a Familiar Sun

Golden rays on fields so wide,
Laughter dances, joy cannot hide.
Breezes whisper secrets near,
In the warmth, we hold dear.

Memories drift like clouds above,
Every heartbeat speaks of love.
Familiar smiles, gentle and bright,
Carried home on wings of light.

Through seasons that come and go,
In this place, our spirits grow.
Time stands still, as shadows play,
Underneath the sun's warm ray.

Nature hums a soothing tune,
Beneath the watchful eye of moon.
Together, we weave our dreams,
In the day's soft golden beams.

Hold my hand, let's wander far,
Hand in hand, we chase a star.
In this warmth, forever run,
Living life under the sun.

Wings of Hope Take Flight

In the stillness of the night,
Dreams awaken, take their flight.
Stars like candles in the sky,
Whispers of what we might try.

Each heartache, a lesson learned,
Through the fire, our spirits burned.
With each struggle, hope ignites,
Wings of love reach new heights.

When shadows fall and spirits fade,
In the darkness, light is made.
A gentle breeze, a guiding hand,
Takes us to a brighter land.

So let us rise on wings of grace,
Together, we'll find our place.
Boundless skies, our hearts align,
In love's embrace, we will shine.

With courage forged in trials faced,
In the heavens, dreams are chased.
With hopeful hearts, we soar so high,
Embracing life, we learn to fly.

Across the Divide of Time

Moments linger, like sweet perfume,
Stories echo in the room.
Past and present intertwine,
In the heart, they brightly shine.

Every tick of the clock reveals,
Emotions raw, and truth that heals.
In the silence, voices call,
Across the divide, we stand tall.

Photographs in colors bright,
Capture dreams that take to flight.
Faces change, but souls remain,
In the dance of joy and pain.

Threads of time, a tapestry,
Woven with our history.
Lessons learned through joy and strife,
In every chapter, lies our life.

So take my hand, let's walk this line,
Through the stories, let us shine.
In every heartbeat, memories chime,
Together we traverse through time.

The Undying Thread

In twilight's glow, our hearts connect,
Unseen ties we can't neglect.
Through every storm and sunny day,
The thread of love will lead the way.

Bound by dreams we dared to share,
In silent moments, love laid bare.
With every whisper, every sigh,
The undying thread will never die.

Through tangled paths, we find our grace,
In each embrace, a warm embrace.
Time may fray, but never cut,
For in our hearts, we stay unstrut.

With laughter shared and tears we've shed,
This thread of trust is softly spread.
A bond that's forged in fire and fate,
In life's grand weave, we resonate.

So hold me close, let's face the night,
With the undying thread as our light.
Together, we write a story rare,
In love's embrace, we find our care.

When the Seasons Align Once More

Beneath the sky of twilight hues,
The whispers dance like morning dew.
As leaves exchange their golden grace,
We find ourselves in this warm place.

When winter's chill begins to fade,
And spring's sweet song begins to play,
A gentle breeze brings forth the light,
Revealing dreams held out of sight.

With every turn the earth will make,
A tapestry of paths we take.
In every season's tender sway,
Love finds its way, night turns to day.

From autumn's chill to summer's heat,
Our hearts align, a perfect beat.
In nature's rhythm, we will find,
The ties that bind, forever kind.

So let us cherish every hour,
As blooms unfold, and moments flower.
For when the seasons come around,
In love's embrace, we are unbound.

The Radiant Pulse of New Affection

In the quiet of a fleeting glance,
Two souls awaken, start to dance.
A spark ignites, an ember glows,
In hidden depths where silence flows.

With each heartbeat, love's rhythm beats,
A melody that softly greets.
The joy that swells within our chest,
In this bright pulse, we feel our best.

Through laughter shared and secrets told,
New affections start to unfold.
Like budding flowers in the spring,
Each moment blooms, our hearts take wing.

A tender touch, a breathless sigh,
In this embrace, we learn to fly.
With every challenge met with grace,
We find our home in each warm space.

As shadows fade and daylight beams,
In the warmth of our shared dreams.
The radiant pulse of love so pure,
Forevermore, with hearts we cure.

In the Soft Glow of Shared Silence

In the evening's calm embrace,
We sit together, face to face.
No words are needed, still we know,
In silence deep, our feelings flow.

A quiet peace that settles in,
Where every heartbeat can begin.
The world outside may press and pound,
But here within, our hearts are found.

Each breath a whisper, soft and clear,
In this ethereal sphere, we steer.
The gentle hush, a sacred space,
In shared silence, we find our place.

Moments linger, time stands still,
In this embrace, we feel the thrill.
A thousand words, yet none are said,
In the soft glow, our souls are wed.

The night will pass, the dawn will break,
But in this stillness, hearts awake.
Together bound, without a sound,
In silence sweet, our love is found.

Hearths and Hearts Anew

When the fire crackles, bright and bold,
It warms the night against the cold.
At hearths aglow, our stories blend,
In laughter shared, our hearts extend.

With every spark that lights the air,
We find a solace, love to share.
In cozy corners, whispers play,
As shadows dance, and moments sway.

Each flicker speaks of hopes and dreams,
Of future paths and vibrant themes.
Together building, brick by brick,
With every hug, our hearts beat thick.

Through seasons turning, life anew,
Our bond grows strong; it's tried and true.
At chilly nights when winds may howl,
We find our peace in every growl.

So let us gather, friend or lover,
In the light of flames, under cover.
For in these hearths, our love is sewn,
Together formed, never alone.

Milton Keynes UK
Ingram Content Group UK Ltd.
UKHW021208261024
450281UK00007B/103